About the Author

Hi, My name is Siddharth Lohani having a rich experience in Digital marketing. My journey started back in 2019 when I got the chance to work for a well-established fitness manufacturer where I had to market gym products to B2B clients. In that company, I got good exposure to SEO, Paid ads, Social media, and ORM. Along with that, I was also doing a part-time job with an online company where my task was to go through FB ads and put my views also was working on improving the search engine algorithms for organic searches. Soon started my own brand Technically open where the main goal was to serve people for their digital marketing needs. Interactions with domestic and foreign clients were a good learning curve for me.

Through this book, I am trying to make you understand Digital marketing in the easiest way possible and give practical tips that can be used to grow digitally.

Table of Contents

Acknowledgement

In this book, you will learn all the fundamentals and the mastery-level tools and functions used in digital marketing. This book not only covers digital marketing but also enhances your knowledge of marketing by talking in brief about some important fundamentals. Through this book, you will be able to crack any digital marketing interview or start your agency with confidence, as it includes a step-by-step guide to help you pave your career. In this edition, all the updated data is provided as 2022–2023 so that the readers don't find it irrelevant. After completing this book.

1. <u>Introduction to Digital Marketing</u>

In today's era, it's more convenient than ever to connect with someone or to gather information about a topic in no time. Thanks to the internet, which has bridged the gap and connected billions worldwide, Wishing someone a happy birthday is now as simple as a click away, as is communicating with customers about one's products or services. Digital media travels at a much greater speed than any other form, and it's easy to use. Helping businesses worldwide unlock their potential

Let's take a look at the scope of digital marketing. But first, let's understand digital marketing in brief.

What is Digital Marketing?

Digital marketing, in simple words, is known as targeted, measurable, and interactive marketing of goods or services using digital technologies to reach out to mass audiences and turn them into paying customers. Digital marketing is also a useful tool to retain customers by communicating valuable information.

Later in this book, we'll go over how digital marketing can help you keep customers.
Some of the defining characteristics of digital marketing are as follows:

Detailed Targeting

Digital marketing gives an upper edge to marketers, as now they can target the audience based on age, gender, location, income, interest, seniority, life events, and much more. This is done to precisely target the audience that can be the right fit. In addition, the CRM data and the re-targeting data are also helpful as they target the right audience.

1. Two-way connect

We have cracked the code of connecting with our audience in order to foster better relationships and encourage the purchase of a product or service in digital marketing. Digital marketing is set to be a two-way communication channel as the audience can engage with the content shared on social sites and web pages. The likes, comments, and shared feedback are some examples. Not only that, but the ability to track the performance of our content or ads using analytic tools is extremely beneficial, and thus these tools are also regarded as a two-way communication channel because they display the metrics.

2. Targeting one

In digital marketing, the targeting of the right audience for the business is just a click away. A platform where ads are hosted digitally collects user marketing data, unlike traditional marketing, to serve them better, and in return, the brand benefits as now they can use the data collected to target the right audience. In digital marketing, unlike traditional marketing, there is no mass promotion without set targeting. Targeting one helps channel businesses' efforts in the right direction.

3. Measurability

In traditional marketing, there was no clear analysis of how well the ad performed and what the conversion was, whereas in digital marketing, you have the power to track and measure the performance and make tweaks to make it more effective, saving cost in the long run. Any digital marketing activity's analytics show how many people saw the ad, how many clicked, what the conversion was, and so on.

4. Push vs Pull

Marketing can be push or pull in nature. Cold calling, bulk emails, bulk messaging, and product testing are examples of push marketing, where you push your products to customers to sell, whereas in pull marketing you just advertise to reach more people and spread awareness about your offerings to attract them to make a purchase.

5. Real time

As digital marketing opens up the ability to track performance, it also has a dashboard to track activities on a real-time basis, from impressions to cost. You can track it all.

Origin of Digital Marketing

The term "digital marketing" was first introduced in 1990, at the start of Web 1.0.

In Web 1.0, users could only gather information and could not interact with it or share it on the internet; this made marketers unsure of their strategies.

Yahoo was the first search engine that was introduced on the world wide web, followed by other small competitors such as Hotspot, Looksmart, and Alexa.

Then, in 1998, Google entered the market, and at the same time, Microsoft also entered the market, wiping out all the small competition. This also gave extra mileage for the implementation of Web 2.0, where users could freely engage with the product or the business, share it on social media, and so on. Now in 2022, we are living in Web 3.0, which has additional features such as AI, NFTS, automated systems, and much more.

To sum up, It was first called as internet marketing or web marketing now it is known as online marketing.

Evolution of marketing

Traditional marketing was once the only way to reach out to new potential customers. In the 1990s, marketing happened through newspaper ads, radio ads, banner ads, poster ads, direct mail, magazines, TV commercials, and direct selling. Not to say that those techniques were bad; after all, there was rarely any other option available at the time.

In the early '20s, the internet became popular, which also led to the popularity of personal computers and other portable digital devices. This causes a significant increase in search engines and social media platforms. Now marketing is much more preferred digitally in the forms of social media ads, search engine ads, influencer marketing, video ads, and much more. To give an example of the potential of digital advertising, Google and Facebook combined have a market cap of $2.5 trillion plus. Digital marketing provides marketers with accurate data that can be measured and used to make changes to get better results, unlike traditional marketing, where the amount of money spent on advertising cannot be controlled or monitored.

A quote by a famous American merchant and a political figure highlights the use of traditional marketing practices.

"Half of the money spent on advertising is wasted and the trouble is, No one knows which half."

Exciting future of Digital Marketing

Digital marketing is the hype, and it is ever-growing. There are almost 30 trends in digital marketing that are going to take over the market, and being up to date-with these trends is a must. These upcoming trends will not only help you secure a better job but if you want to establish a business in the future, they are guaranteed to come in handy. Some of the major trends that are seen on daily basis are the utilization of short videos this means that the attention span of an individual is reducing, That translates as a marketer we have to send their message as short and crisply as possible. Similarly in daily updates more and more users are now consuming easy-to-read short content that gives the proper gist of the news. Also, we can see that metaverse can open up new horizons to digital marketing where marketers have to think creatively. Influencer marketing is also something that you need to work on as businesses are switching to niche influencers. Trends in digital marketing are endless with new updates something new pops up and you have to adapt to it.

2. <u>Fundamentals of Digital Marketing</u>

In this chapter, we will touch upon some of the core principles of digital marketing and how to efficiently use them. This chapter not only focuses on digital marketing but also has some pointers that can be used to make an offline marketing event successful.

SEO (Search Engine Optimization)

The most trending topic that comes to almost all marketers, as well as businesses, is SEO (search engine optimization). Although the term might look very technical, believe me, it's not that hard. After going through this book, you will be confident about search engine optimization and how it works.

Some fundamental knowledge about SEO

Search Engine Optimization, by its name, signifies that the process of optimizing a website includes technical optimization, link popularity, and content relevance. to make the page more findable, popular, and most relevant to user search queries. As a result, the page is highly ranked by the search engine.

Search Engine Optimization (SEO) is not rocket science. Most digital marketers and business owners tend to do it the wrong way, which results in poor results. Search engine optimization should be done systematically, following each step, and not by doing multiple steps in a single go.

SEO is the undisputed king of digital marketing. 98% of all internet users (smartphones, laptops, desktops, and other smart devices) use a search engine at least once a month. Not only that, Google alone processes around 63,000 search queries per second, which total approximately 90720000 per day. But the data shows that 63% of all the searches are for local areas, such as "Hair salons near me" and "Care Repair Shops in My Area." This gives the marketer some extra room to work on the SEO of the website and the local business listing.

A local business listing is essential for any business, big or small. SEO can be done on local business listings as well to make them appear higher on the search page. This can be done by properly optimizing the listing and adding relevant content.

Anything that is on the internet and can be indexed is eligible for SEO.

PPC (Pay-Per-Click)

Pay Per Click is a well-known term among the majority of marketers, and PPC has proven to be more effective than SEO in the short term. Yes, short term, as in PPC, the business injects money to rank higher and gain visibility, but as soon as the company stops the PPC campaign, the ranking drops and the site receives no visitors or leads. SEO is the first fundamental activity to be completed before PPC because in PPC, you rank a keyword and it is generally bid wisely—the higher your PPC bid, the higher your visibility, and vice versa. Doing PPC without investing resources in SEO is a big no, as SEO ensures the site is optimized for the user and that keywords are relevant and indexed. PPC can surely boost your SEO efforts, as users will land on the page, and if it is structured properly, they might even browse further.

Pay per click is available across all search engines, and Google is the most popular one as it accounts for the highest number of searches. In pay per click, you pick a keyword or a set of keywords, choose the right demographic to target, and link your landing page. Google keywords need to be relevant to the product or service that you are offering. With keyword research available on Google Ads, you can choose the right keyword for your campaign.

PPC can give you amazing results only if you have chosen the right keywords relevant to your product or service and have placed a good bid. Yes, to ensure that you are getting the right output from PPC website optimization, a good bid is necessary. Apart from that, a good bid can help you see better results, as most of the other marketers do everything right but don't keep the bid price as per the prediction by Google's keyword planner, thus losing all their budget in impressions. They lose money because not putting in the right bid makes their PPC ad rank lower than other competitors.

A low PPC bid can result in your ad being shown on the bottom of page 1 or maybe on page 2, and so on. It's a good practice to place the bid according to the Google keyword planner's estimations.

Social Media

The most important topic that every digital marketer should be aware of is social media. It began as a trend in which people could share details about their personal lives via photos, videos, or blogging. Different social media platforms have different demographics (gender, age, and location).

Let's talk about Instagram. Modern-day marketers feel that Instagram is the king of social media, and if they can generate traffic over the platform, it will surely improve the company's sales figures. That statement is partially correct because it's true you get a relatively large user base to target on Instagram, which can have a huge impact on sales, but Instagram is generally used by millennials and not by other groups in general. This means that if the product or service is related to millennials, then only marketers can see a positive trend by leveraging Instagram.

Instagram gives a plethora of options to digital marketers to create content, which includes static posts, videos, IGTV, Instagram Live, stories, and Reel. This form of content gives the marketer more ideas as to how to portray the business or service using Instagram.

Facebook

It is without a doubt the best social media platform available, with more useful features than other platforms. Features of Facebook include static posting, video (short and long format), textual posts, group posts, stories, live, and games. Facebook is still a relevant tool for marketers who want to target people who are in the 30-plus age group, as they are more comfortable using Facebook than any other platform. Facebook can be used as a great platform to reach high-paying populations. This group of people has more purchasing power than millennials, which translates into high sales.

On Facebook, you can join groups that are related to your business niche and have a targeted audience. Groups allow you to reach a larger number of users who are not following you directly but are members of the group.

YouTube

Google purchased Youtube for $1.6 million in 2006, completely altering the business model. Earlier, Youtube's only revenue stream was advertisements, but now it also hosts paid video content and offers premium memberships to its users. YouTube can be a good marketing tool only if the marketer follows the set strategies. What are those strategies? We will touch on this in detail in the next few chapters.

Youtube is also a great tool to be used for SEO, as Google gives priority to its medium first, and creating YouTube videos with the right keywords in the title and the description can help boost the ranking. There is a lot of stuff you can do for SEO on Youtube.

Pinterest

It's a widely popular social media tool generally used by females, and it's mostly used by millennials. Pinterest can be a perfect match for any kind of business as it drives traffic and also helps with SEO. Unlike other platforms on Pinterest, you can't host live and stories, but its video feature and pin feature steal the show. Also, the algorithm of Pinterest is top-notch, as it refers only to relevant posts for the user. Making a pin with the right set of keywords and an image or video relevant to your target audience can give you really rich results.

LinkedIn

Both as a marketer and as an employee, LinkedIn is a gold mine. For marketers, if the business is B2B, then using LinkedIn is considered to be the best choice among any other platforms because the decision-makers of the company generally use Linkedin, and getting those people to engage with your post can nurture prosperous B2B relations and guarantee you better sales. On LinkedIn, various types of content can be posted, ranging from static, carousel, blog, video, stories, and polls. LinkedIn can also help with SEO; more on that later.

If you are a freelancer or looking for a job, it's a great tool as you can optimize your profile and join relevant groups to get the latest updates. Similarly, if you are a marketer for a B2B business, LinkedIn should be your top priority, as through it you can reach other businesses either through your company page, organic postings, ads, or postings on niche-specific groups.

Twitter

The most unique feature of Twitter is that all accounts are publicly visible; there is no such thing as a private account where only after you accept a request can the user see your post. Twitter is a micro-blogging social media platform where there are certain limits on the word count, especially when you are using hyperlinks. Twitter can be a great platform to communicate with customers, though it is seen as the hub of politics and celebrity gossip.

On Twitter, there is an option to post images, videos, or stories too, but the dimensions are different from the standard 800 px by 800 px.

Other social media platforms include Snapchat, minds, twitch, ello, and many more. These platforms can be a great asset for creating user engagement and for SEO purposes.

Remember to be active on all the main platforms mentioned above, as this will ensure that your brand has a 360-degree presence in the market and that customers searching for your business will gain some credibility if they see your presence. All social media platforms are designed to help you connect with people by sharing your thoughts through any type of media or plain text, but remember that social media favors normal users more than business pages, and this can result in less reach for your post. There is a way out, which we discuss in the next chapter.

Video marketing

We're all addicted to video content because it's simple to understand and visually appealing. In video marketing, the best strategy is to create a video ad or any video that is based on storytelling, as it acts as a hook to attract more viewers and is also highly shared. Video marketing can be done organically as well as paid; organically, the marketers use platforms such as YouTube, Facebook, IGTV, and Linked In, as they give the highest view rate compared to any other platform. In this book, you will learn more about video marketing, from creating a video from scratch to publishing it on the internet in both organic and paid ways.

SEO (Search engine optimization)

In general, SEO involves ranking on the front page of Google and other search engines, though it's not that easy. In SEO, you need to ensure that you are publishing only quality content on your site because search engines favor quality content. This might raise the question of what is quality content. Any content that is clear to understand and is unique with accurate insights is considered to be quality content. Though search engines have algorithms in place to identify quality content, they prefer sites with more views because it demonstrates how trustworthy the content is in terms of the site; it also indicates that this is trending content for the keyword entered by the user.

To perform SEO, you must have a proper strategy in place before starting to work. These strategies include sites for backlinking, keywords to target, off-page requirements, on-page requirements, an SEO checklist, and analytic tools. Once you are prepared with the things mentioned, you are set to start search engine optimization and deliver good results.

P-O-E-M Framework

To help you with your activities, The main aim of this framework is to help you set the right strategies for your marketing activities, which include paid media, earned media, and owned media.

Paid media:

As the name suggests, it is a form of marketing that includes an upfront cost. In simple words, it is the paid media used for advertising a good or service. It includes ads on display networks over the internet such as Facebook, Google, Yahoo, LinkedIn, Twitter and others. Paid media is thought to be more effective in terms of generating good results because it is well-targeted and ads are purchased on a daily basis.

Owned media:

It is considered an asset to the company, i.e., the company's website, Facebook page, LinkedIn page, Twitter account, and so on. It also includes all the apps by the company on IOS or the play store. Similarly, it also accounts for the company's creatives, videos, and content. Owned media is good for the long term as the results take

time, but the output generated is better than paid media.

Earned media:

It is organic and unpaid media. This type of media includes publicity generated through word of mouth and recommendations. Earned media also includes social media signals such as the number of likes, shares, favorites, comments, re-tweets, etc. Earned media is typically generated by users, making it more credible and a useful tool for marketers to target specific audiences.

Conclusion: The combination of all three methods mentioned above is set to be the best practice for any marketer who wants to promote a brand or business.

3. <u>Facebook</u>

<u>A brief background of Facebook</u>

Wonders happen in the best places, Similllary the modern marvel was first started at Harvard University, USA. In its early stages, Facebook was only an internal network connecting Harvard University students. It was founded in 2003 by Harvard University students Mark Zuckerberg, Dustin Moskovitz, Eduardo Saverin, and Chris Huges. It is now, as we all know, a component of meta platforms.

Meta will now be recognized as the parent corporation of Facebook, Instagram, Whatsapp, and Oculus, among other things. Mark Zuckerberg, the founder, and CEO of Facebook has stated his desire to create the Metaverse, a virtual environment in which individuals may do almost anything, including work, play, and socialize.

(Facebook's first version)

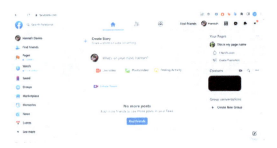

(Facebook's Latest version)

The new version

Facebook has updated its UI to serve its users more efficiently. Here we can see there have been a lot of add-on made by the Facebook team such as marketplace, groups, messenger, and so on. Facebook will continue to change its UI in order to serve its users more efficiently.

Facebook's clean UI makes it easy to perform daily tasks on the platform being it sending friend requests, checking notifications, messaging, scrolling feed, and posting.

Facebook algorithm

Ever wonder why you only see limited posts and stories on Facebook and not from all your friends? For example, we assume you have 500 friends on Facebook, but you don't have them. see all posts by them. The reason for this is that Facebook doesn't want to bombard you with posts and make you less interested in scrolling further. This will cause them a lot of problems because the platform's main purpose is to show you ads, and if you don't stay on the platform, it will go against their business model.

Let's welcome the "Edgerank Algorithm." In simple words, it's the name of the algorithm that determines what to prioritize in your feed and makes all the boring content hidden or at the bottom of your feed to make you less overwhelmed and get all the information about your friends in just a few glances. The Edgerank algorithm handles all types of content, including posts, comments, stories, and videos.

$$\sum_{edges\ e} u_e w_e d_e$$

u_e ~ affinity score between viewing user and edge creator
W_e ~ weight for this edge type (create, connect, like, tag, ect.)
d_e ~ time decay factor based on how long ago the edge was created

How does Edgerank work?

(To keep it simple, silly) Edgerank can be regarded as a credit rating that is unique to every user and no one except Facebook knows how it works. But for my readers, I got some insights from past Facebook conferences that talk about this algorithm a bit.

- ➢ Affinity Score
- ➢ Edge Weight
- ➢ Time Decay

➢ Affinity score

It is a relational score that gives signals to the edge rank on how to arrange the user feed. It is calculated based on one factor that has too many actions. Yes, you guessed it right it's the engagement that includes liking, clicking, commenting, messaging, friending, and other similar engagement-rich actions. So basically, if you have shown engagement with your friend's post/story or with the account, it will signal to Facebook what has to be a priority and what shouldn't be.

Similarly, it works for any business page content if the user has engaged with it recently; otherwise, it will be at the bottom.

➢ Edge weight

Every Facebook post is assigned a weight, indicating its importance. In other words, a remark on your post may be more valuable than a "like" or "share." Facebook modifies the edge weights to reflect the type of content it believes users will find most interesting.

➤ <u>Time decay</u>

Every piece of content you share on Facebook, whether it's a story, post, video, or anything else, has a 24-hour lifespan. So the algorithm favors the most recent content and pushes it down the page as time passes, and after 24 hours it's hard to show on the news feed as it's somewhere at the bottom.

Let's talk more about Facebook and its business features.

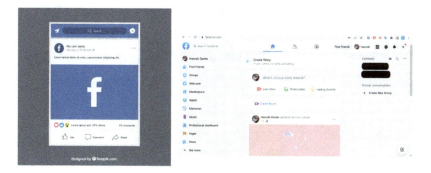

(Freepik, Facebook)

We all have used this feature to connect with our friends; it allows you to add people to your contact list so that every time you post, it's on their feed. But Facebook has updated its algorithm so that it only lets the most engaging followers see your content first then based on the activity received it is distributed to others. Currently, the algorithm works by distributing content to less than 1% of users, and if the engagement is above 60%, it is shown to the less than or equal to 1% audience. A Facebook friend list can be an excellent source for inbound marketing because you can connect with like-minded people who have indicated an interest in your offerings and then share content, and exclusive offers with them or directly chat with them. They say modern problems require modern solutions, so why not use Facebook in a different way to market it to the right audience? Remember not to overdo adding people, as adding people you have no mutual friends with can lead to the suspension of your account.

The 3'E strategy

The 3'E strategy used on Facebook or any social media platform

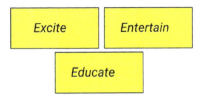

1. <u>Excite:</u> The content posted on the platform need to be attractive enough to grab the attention of the audience and should relate to the target audience.

2. <u>Entertain:</u> Content that is posted on the platform should be entertaining enough to engage with the audience and act like a hook for the audience.

3. <u>Educate:</u> Just entertainment and no value might not always work as audiences on these platforms are smarter now they want to trade their time in exchange for something valuable.

In conclusion, I would like to add every marketer should follow the 3'E strategy but should keep in mind that each platform serves different audiences. For example, what works on LinkedIn may not work well on Facebook, and vice versa.

The campaign objective

It's more than just necessary, before executing any campaign, to define all the objectives that you have in mind. The ACC method is the most effective way to check all of the boxes.

A stand for awareness C stand for consideration and the other C stand for conversion

The awareness stage can be built using multiple ways: by collaborating with influencers, posting organically, running ads, starting offers, or by word of mouth. It is generally done by the brands so that people remember their business; that's why they show up multiple times.

The consideration stage is when the prospect develops an interest to buy the product/offering. This also includes any action taken by the user such as sharing their contact information or signing up for a newsletter.

The concert stage is the ultimate goal of any campaign, be it organic or paid, as this is the end goal that the brand wants. Here, the prospect purchases the product/offering from the brand.

Organic features that you can utilize as a user or business include

➢ Messaging

I don't want to emphasize messaging more, as we all know it is one of the most used features on Facebook. Through messaging, you can connect with customers, friends, pages, and other audiences. There are different settings you might want to explore further, as just like our emails Facebook also has this filter to remove spam and new contacts we didn't add.

In messages, the first UI shows the primary inbox and the option to the right-hand corner opens up message requests similarly it also shows open spam. Remember to check them both every week because if you are running a business on Facebook it can make you lose some potential leads.

> **Notifications**

Your every new update deserves engagement, so you will see it all, whether it's a like, comment, friend request, event, or unseen message.

> **Friend request:**

In this section, you can find out who you know and also see Facebook recommendations to send requests instantly.

There is a strategy to help your business grow using this feature; for a detailed explanation, refer to the last section of this chapter.

➢ **Marketplace:**

It is a platform where you can list your products or offers, choose the right category, and use the right keywords.

Facebook Marketplace

In the marketplace, you can list the offering with your mobile number and other relevant details for free, but this is limited, as Facebook says that to gain more reach, you have to run marketplace ads.

➢ **Groups:**

It is a like-minded community of people sharing the same interest. People join Facebook groups because it provides them with content they enjoy and allows them to interact with other users who share their interests. It is helpful as you can create an event, polls, discussions, and similar things.

This can be used for business, as businesses can share their posts on these groups in their niche and garner a new audience and increase.

Paid marketing

Integrating paid marketing into your campaign makes your business reach out to a greater number of audiences faster and builds awareness among them at a much greater speed compared to organic.

Paid marketing can be done on Facebook through ads, and it's not as difficult as you think, but yes, ads are getting more competitive day after day as more and more new businesses are leveraging them. In ads, you get to target the right audience based on their age, gender, location, interests, and behavior, making it the most convenient feature available on Facebook to reach the right set of audiences.

Now you have to be smart enough to check if your competitors are using Facebook ads, and if they are, you need to analyze if they are lead generation ads, website traffic, or page likes. This will help you pick the right budget for your ads. If you choose a lower budget, your ad might not reach as many people as your competition is trying to reach.

To check if your competition ads are running on Facebook, follow the following steps.

Step 1: Go to the competition page and click on "page transparency" (visible on the left side of the Facebook web version).

Step 2: Click on go to ad library.

Step 3: Analyze the type of ads currently running by the company and on which platforms they run.

Anatomy of Facebook ads

While setting up ads on Facebook, there is a structure one must follow. The structure includes an ad campaign, Ad set, and Ads.

Ad campaign

Here you have to set your final goal through the campaign this can be getting more page likes, leads, app installs, website visits, etc. Further, the ad is defined in the next two stages.

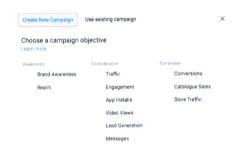

Ad set

At this stage the business defines the budget, days to run, targeting, scheduling, placements, etc. All of the mentioned things work together in such a way that they fulfill the company's objective. An ad campaign on Facebook can have multiple ad sets.

Ad

This is what the audience sees on Facebook. It has to include an ad creative, video, and an image, along with a compelling caption, to attract the audience. The design of the ad is considered crucial for grabbing customers' attention.

Facebook ads

The most useful tool for marketers is Facebook ads and it has just got better in Meta as it has a new UI and business tools.

➢ Business tools

You might be surprised if I told you that you can directly post from Facebook to Instagram and track all of your insights in one place. Sounds amazing, right?

Yes with the introduction of business tools now you can post on both platforms at once also you can schedule them to publish them at a later date. In business tools, you can directly boost ads choose the platform, set a budget, and much more. To use it at its very best you need to add your Instagram business account to your Facebook page then only this feature is unlocked.

➢ Ads manager

One of the best platforms to run ads is none other than Facebook. The acquisition cost is comparatively low and quite reasonable compared to other platforms. On Ads Manager, you can set ads for lead generation, app promotion, boosting website traffic, selling eCommerce products, and retargeting.

There are different forms in which ads can be run

The standard picture just like your regular Facebook post 1080x1080 px is size.

Carousel media if you want to add more than one picture and want the call to action on every image the size is the same 1080x1080 px

For video ads 1080x1080 px. From Ads Manager, you can do more as it gives you access to some of the tools you won't find elsewhere. For starters, one of the most used is the audience tool, as it helps in setting up the audience as per the ad that we are going to run. In audience creation, we can choose the location, age, gender, and interests, and exclude interests (to narrow down further).

Always remember that the narrower your audience, the better the ads will perform; however, keeping it medium will cost you more and reduce the number of leads. Furthermore, in Facebook ads, you can use pixels, which are a tool that aids in retargeting all those who have previously visited your site.

For more details on it go to www.technicallyopen.com.

Steps and explanation to set up ads on Facebook

➢ <u>Step 1:</u> Go to Facebook ads, as the feature provided in the meta Facebook dashboard is limited and ads need a more detailed application.

To go to ads manager simply add the URL:
https://bit.ly/adsmanagerbook.

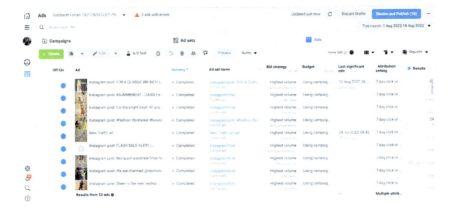

(Facebook ads manager page)

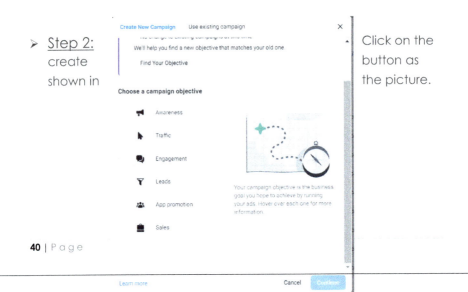

> **Step 2:**
> create
> shown in

Create New Campaign   Use existing campaign   ×

We'll help you find a new objective that matches your old one.

Find Your Objective

Choose a campaign objective

📢 Awareness

➤ Traffic

💬 Engagement

▼ Leads

👥 App promotion

💼 Sales

Your campaign objective is the business goal you hope to achieve by running your ads. Hover over each one for more information.

Click on the
button as
the picture.

Learn more   Cancel   Continue

As you can see here, you have to choose your objective, which defines the goal of your ad campaign.

For demo purposes, we have taken lead generation as our objective.

No, you have to name your campaign to make it easy to recognize, as any business prefers to run more than one ad at a time to leverage the power of paid media.

> Step 3: Next, you go to "ad set" Here, you have to give it a name and then choose the Facebook page you want to run ads for. Remember, it's advised to connect your Instagram account to your Facebook page. The process is really easy, and it helps as you are spending the same per day but ads are visible across both platforms. It reacts to connecting your Instagram with

Facebook; just go to the page settings and add an Instagram account.

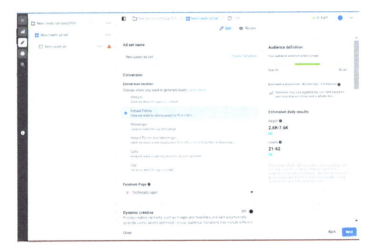

In the ad set at the very beginning, you have to choose the type of conversion you want from your ads; here we are using lead generation as an example, There are various options available such as instant forms, instant forms and messenger, phone call, website, and messenger. Based on your selection, the CTA button will direct the targeted user to capture their lead.

Just below that you have to choose the Facebook page that you want to use to run ads. Make sure you select the right page for the campaign as this can make it ineffective.

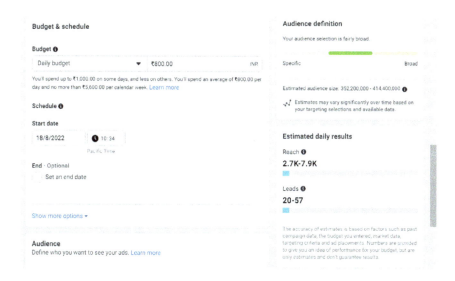

Here you have to enter the budget you want to set for the campaign. In this, you can set a daily budget or a lifetime budget and also schedule the campaign. Pro tip: Always refer to the sidebar, as shown in the image, as it gives an estimate of how many leads can be expected; similarly, for website clicks, it depicts the same.

Show more options ▾

Audience

Define who you want to see your ads. Learn more

Create new audience   Use saved audience ▾

Custom Audiences   Create new ▾

Q Search existing audiences

Exclude

Locations

Location:
- India

Age

18 - 65+

Gender

All genders

Detailed targeting

All demographics, interests and behaviours

Advantage Detailed Targeting: ✦
- Off

Languages

All languages

Show more options ▾

Save This Audience

Audience definition

Your audience selection is fairly broad.

Specific ──────────────●─────── Broad

Estimated audience size: 352,200,000 - 414,400,000 ⓘ

⟋ Estimates may vary significantly over time based on
your targeting selections and available data

Estimated daily results

Reach ❶
2.7K-7.9K

Leads ❶
20-57

The accuracy of estimates is based on factors such as past
campaign data, the budget you entered, market data,
targeting criteria and ad placements. Numbers are provided
to give you an idea of performance for your budget but are
only estimates and don't guarantee results.

Now coming to the audience section, it is important to reach out to the right group base of people to make the campaign more effective. You can choose a saved audience or create one using the tab shown.The audience lets you define the demography you want to target.

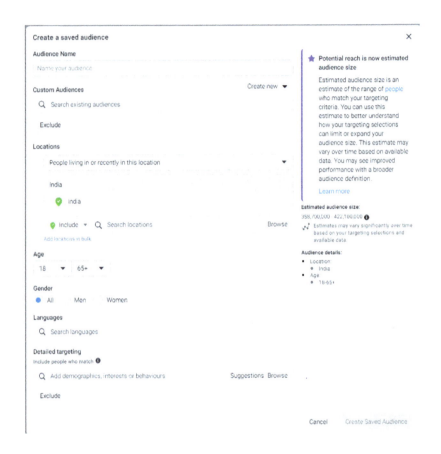

You have to enter the locations you want to target, followed by age, gender, and language based on your targeted audience. Below you have detailed targeting which is helpful as it reaches those people who are interested in a similar product or service to that for which you are campaigning. In the detailed targeting, you also get the option to target based on demographics and behavior.

Demographics

As depicted in the image in this section, you can choose from education, finances, life events, parents, and relationships and work to further narrow down your audience. This is helpful as it makes the ad more relevant to the user, but it also has a drawback. On Facebook, not all businesses update their about info, thus making the ad reach fewer users and making the cost go up.

Behaviors

In this, we can target the user based on their interaction with Facebook

4. Instagram

A short story on Instagram

Kevin Systrom is the creator of Burbn, a multi-featured HTML5 prototype for check-ins. He showed it to investors, who were impressed with his concept. He received $500,000 in financing. Mike and Systrom Rieger turned the prototype into a product. They eventually chose to focus completely on photo sharing on mobile phones, and get rid of all the

more features On October 6, 2010, the product, renamed Instagram, was released on the App Store.

Everyone who registers for an Instagram account has a profile and a news feed, much like on Facebook or Twitter.

Instagram is a useful tool that displays any images or videos you publish on your profile. Your posts are only visible to those individuals who follow you in their news feeds. You also receive timely updates from the people you follow.

Instagram works similar to a Facebook that places a focus on mobile use and visual sharing. Similar to other social media platforms, you may communicate with other users by following them, allowing others to follow you, commenting, liking, tagging, and sending private messages. Additionally, Instagram photographs can be saved.

There is a lot to learn about Instagram, so here is some useful information to help you get started on the social networking site.

That was too bookish knowledge… Simply put, it is a growing platform designed for the general public to share their experiences with their friends and family. But recent advancements and changes in the digital ecosystem made this giant think more about making it available for commercial use.

We've all seen that it's quite easy to make a profile on Instagram with just a few simple taps. Enter your right information, authenticate it with your number as email creation might ban your account (Instagram thinks it's spam), and it's done. According to online articles and some hands-on testing, the most recent update requires you to take a selfie of yourself to create an account. At the time this was written, it was under beta testing and will be available soon for users.

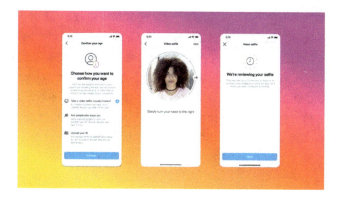

(source TechCrunch)

The best thing about Instagram is that it is constantly evolving and outperforming its competitors. A great example would be the introduction of the Instagram reel. Though we can say it was a lookalike of a similar platform that was trending, here it made more sense as Instagram already has 1 billion monthly active users worldwide and the introduction of a 30-second short video on their platform was required to retain them.

Instagram Strategies

Let's talk about some of the marketing strategies you can use on Instagram

Hashtags: Like SEO for search engines is done similarly hashtags are chosen for Instagram posts. Yes, this gives the post the required boost and reaches more people however it's vital to use only relevant hashtags that relate to your page or post and not use hashtags such as #love #likeforlike #like similar to these the reason is simple Instagram can detect whether hashtags are relevant to the post share also the use of banned hashtags can lead to serious implications.

It is preferred to use not more than 12 hashtags on a post or 15 on a reel however it varies and you can try experimenting to find the sweet spot.

A strategy I often use for hashtags is I don't use super trending hashtags that have <4m posts whereas I use hashtags with>1 m posts. So I have a bucket where I put 6 longtail hashtags to be precise that have posts under 200k and the next set of 4 medium hashtags that have posts ranging between 300k to 500k and the rest 2 hashtags I prefer more than 1 million posts. However the selection of hashtags depends on the offering the business has and the number of hashtags required can differ suppose my business is very niche and hashtags in my category have no more than 10k posts so I'll explore more I can expand, use all categories hashtags, or for example, I have to target more countries ill use more hashtags.

Geo-location tag: It is neglected by many but allows you to get popular in the area you want to attract more audience. Also, it helps find your local business as people search for a location on Instagram, and you are highly likely to appear on the location tag.

Stories: Most of you might think it wasn't required to add stories in the marketing strategy as it is mostly used for inbound marketing (not reaching non-followers). Well to some extent that is right but there is a hidden trick you can use to make stories perform better and attract new customers for starters if you make sure to engage with similar niche audience chances are that they will visit your profile and view your story thus this can be a great trick, similarly if you share something helpful or relevant chances are that your existing followers might share it further in their network and when we put highlights from our previous stories it adds up to making our profile more appealing.

Engagement: I have pitched this a million times to people I have worked for and my colleagues, "Instagram is a two-way platform". You just can't expect that you will post and post and get engagement. To attract a new audience and to help the algorithm you need to post and make sure to like and comment on posts that are of your niche also remember to engage with your existing followers. Engaging with the existing followers might not sound wise as we have to look for new followers but in actual Instagram, the algorithm is quite harsh to decode so the more you are engaged with your followers be it Dm's, likes, comments, tagging and save Instagram favors it and keeps you at the top of their feed. Being on top ensures you will get engagement also it signals to Instagram ago that a post is good as it is being liked so it is passed on to non-followers.

Reel: If you haven't started yet then you should as the reel is potentially the mainstream media for all IG users these days. The reel also gives you an exponentially greater reach compared to regular content. This is because IG wants to promote its reel feature and attract more audience later it can monetize when they get a good amount of users watching the reel on daily basis.

IGTV: Not many are currently using this feature but it can be a go-to for content creators and brands. In this, you are required to upload a video that is more than 30 seconds to 1 minute. Although it's not visible on Instagram as a different section that's because now long format videos can be uploaded directly on the posts section and slowly Instagram is trying to display all long format videos on reels so you can see some long videos too on reels. But if you go live and save the video it will show on Instagram earlier it was IGTV but still it can help in content creation.

Guides: It was reported back in the early 2020s that Instagram is soon shifting towards becoming the next search engine, Users are just required to add a keyword and they will be shown results such as accounts, posts, tags, and places. Guides help to organize the posts and narrate a story or explain the posts better. It is like a blog on Instagram and it can be leveraged for SEO as you can add keywords to the article.

Paid Ads/ Post boosts

Instagram is decreasing its reach as it has to make money through advertising. Using Ads you can reach more audiences faster and in a more targeted way. There are two types of setups available for Instagram ads, mainly through the app and Facebook Ads Manager.

Facebook Ads Manager is preferred as the best medium, as it provides more detailed targeting options with a much more detailed forecast of the ad. The second option is not recommended, but you can use the in-app boost post option, which allows you to boost a specific post based on the demographics you enter using a phone and set the budget.

Setting boost post on mobile

Step1: Select the post you want to boost/ run ads on. Then you have to tap on the Boost post button.

Step 2: Set a goal: Here you are required to pick the preferred goal you want to achieve from the ads it can be more profile visits, more website visits, or more messages this is dependent on your business needs.

Step 3: Choose the target audience: As mentioned on the phone, it is not so easy to set the audience, but you can do some basic edits or go for the automatic audience, which means that based on your followers' interests, more people will be exposed to the ad having similar interests.

Step 4: Set the budget: At the very end you are required to set the budget and the total number of days you want the campaign to run.

Hashtags

A quick question for you what are Instagram captions? ...... Some might just say it a textual content describing the creative, and a good caption might also have a CTA (call-to-action).

But that's not all; on Instagram, you also need to add hashtags to your captions to increase visibility. Here is why? Hashtags can act as a specific keywords that make it easy for users to search or can hint at the Instagram algorithm about the type of content and your niche for better reach.

The use of hashtags can be tricky. some argue that 30 hashtags should be their paper post to increase visibility. Some say to use the first comment to add all your hashtags. Some might say to use the most popular hashtags like #instagood, and others.

But the factual information is that no set figure can work wonders, so you can use hashtags as many as you want but limit them to 20 because using 30 tags for your posts frequently might cause Instagram to flag your account or spam you. Additionally, being shadow banned can be dangerous.

Shadow banned

It is a way Instagram penalizes accounts for not complying with the guidelines given by Instagram or for engaging in spam activities. Shadow ban simply means that your content does not reach out to the audiences that you are targeting by limiting your reach on hashtags. It can also make your content available on your followers' feeds at the very bottom or make it completely disappear from their feed. To limit this, it is required to not indulge in shameful activities such as bulk DMs, using too many hashtags, posting too much, changing your profile name or ID too frequently, having no display image for your profile, and so on.

Hashtags density

There is no set golden figure for the number of hashtags to be used, but from my personal experience and some research, here are the appropriate hashtags to add depending on the form of the content posted. However, keep in mind that these figures are general and may vary depending on the industry or niche.

Post/Video/Reel

You need to divide hashtags based on relevance, popularity, and low-engaging hashtags. For posts, be they carousel or static, you should use no more than 20 hashtags per post. Keep in mind that these hashtags should be relevant to your brand or the content posted; otherwise, they won't give you optimal results.

Dividing hashtags

You are now aware that only relevant hashtags that are limited to 20 in number are considered to be optimal, keeping in mind that 20 hashtags give a brand good exposure on Instagram's feed, explore, or hashtag page.

Though, as stated earlier, it is important to put hashtags in a post based on their popularity, this can be done by doing the research beforehand. You need to use hashtags that have more than 1 million posts and limit them to 3 to 4, then go for medium hashtags that are in the range of 100k to 500k and limit them to 10, and following that, use low hashtags that have posts under 100k. This strategy will give you good and consistent results. Following this hashtag strategy can increase your chances of getting your post in the Explore section of Instagram, as using this strategy will make a ladder for you to climb. First, you will appear on the low hashtags as the top posts, followed by medium and high.

Additional tips for Instagram

➤ Keep changing the hashtags for every new post as using the same hashtags on every post can lead to shadow ban by Instagram also it is considered to be a red flag.

➤ Try to strike up a conversation in the comments section as this will boost your engagement and the algorithm for the post you shared. Instagram will see it as a post that is getting engagement and thus will promote it further to other audiences of similar interests and rank it on hashtags for visibility.

➤ Get as much engagement as possible in the first 1 hour of posting. The Instagram algorithm works differently as it has to accommodate more than 9 million posts per day. To give fair chance to all it has made its algorithm in such a way that it serves the right audience at the right time.

➤ Engage with a new follower as it helps to be on the top of the new user's field. Yes, if someone follows you then you have to make sure your posts are seen by the user, to do so a simple like on their pictures, comment, or DM can show Instagram that users are mutually interested and thus will also prefer to show your content at the top the users feed.

➤ Upload the story of the post uploaded/shared. Stories have a greater reach among our followers. The Instagram algorithm works this way: The posy is shown to a random 10% of people from your follower's list then based on their engagement it will be pushed forward this implies that your post will be visible to the next 10% of your followers and will start to appear on their news feeds in the second or third number. Also with more engagement, your post will be shown on explore page and rank among the top posts of the hashtags chosen.

Update for 2023 on Instagram

The discontinuation of hashtags: Yes, Instagram's latest update is still under development and has been seen by a fortunate few. Add topics is the new update or can be called so, in this you will get a wide variety of options to choose a topic and this will eliminate hashtags as the algorithm tries to be more sophisticated by letting the user decide the topic to recommend it to the audience interested in such topics.

Though it does not mean the total end of hashtags, it is clear that users might need to limit their hashtags to 4 or a maximum of 5 if they use this feature.

Also, remember to pick the right topic while posting, as the algorithm acts like a computer and forms the image by looking at the content posted on hashtags and captions.

5. Linkedin

LinkedIn, as we all know, is a professional social media platform, unlike Facebook or Instagram. Here you share professional life events such as joining a new job, your education, work experience, an article, or a relevant resource from which your connections can get some insightful information.

On LinkedIn, there is no such thing as endless scrolling, which means if you are posting, it should be precise and resourceful, as professionals there don't intend to waste time on the platform. Posting relevant and useful content helps, as it increases your engagement and helps to grow on the platform.

It is also called an online cv essential if you are applying for jobs. That statement is right as you can detail your experience, education, achievements, and much more. As per statistics, there are over 610 million users on LinkedIn spread across 200 countries, which translates into making LinkedIn the 15th most popular emerging platform after Instagram, Facebook, and Snapchat.

(Linkedin UI)

Uses of the Platform

1. Connecting with users: It can be connecting with other B2B clients through your company page, or it can be connecting with work colleagues for professional relation.

2. Receiving recommendations and endorsements from your network. It can help to showcase your skills to the potential employer.

3. An online identity such as a resume where your potential clients or employer can learn more about you.

4. Great tool to market to B2B customers where you can make a business page and showcase your offerings.

5. A good platform for SEO back-linking.

6. Connecting to groups where you can have a knowledge transfer, seek for an opportunity, or promote your product or service.

7. Job hunting platform candidates can find out jobs on the platform as some of the companies prefer to advertise for their job over linkedin. Also on linkedin you get an option to easily apply for jobs and the process is quite easy.

Linkedin algorithms

On LinkedIn, there is a structured algorithm that defines the performance of the post. This also defines the reach of your post on LinkedIn and whether it will be delivered to the users you want to target.

Your content will be classified by the LinkedIn bot into three categories:

➢ **Spam:** You can get past this stage by using good grammar, good quality, and limited links, and limiting your posting frequency.

➢ **Low-quality:** To get past this stage, use a combination of general and niche hashtags. Formatting is essential for making text easier to read. LinkedIn also recommends mentioning outbound links only in comments, not in posts.

➢ **Clear:** Once you've reached the clear stage, look at when your followers are online. Always reply back to your audience to maintain engagement. It's best to avoid editing the post because it reduces its reach.

The algorithm acts as a medium of delivering your content on the platform, as LinkedIn has so many users and processes so much content that it is next to impossible to show all that is posted, so it has to follow some standards. Remember to post only relevant and insightful content curated for professionals if you want to get a better reach.

LinkedIn Groups

It is seen that LinkedIn is sometimes filled with information that may or may not be that useful for the user, and the impact of getting spam or low reach by the algorithm is something we can't work on. But there is a solution that can help you reach out to the right audience with your product or service, or you can have a dedicated place where there are like-minded people and the exchange of information is both useful and purposeful. Yes, here I am talking about LinkedIn groups.

Through groups, one can leverage them and build their network and can also connect with a community to find relevant opportunities.

Which LinkedIn groups should you join?

- ➤ **Size of the group:** If the main objective of your content strategy is to reach out to as many people as possible then group size isn't your concern. But if your content strategy wants to reach a niche targeted audience to make an impact then it is important to look out for small size groups. In smaller groups, there are more engagement among the members, and they are generally more active than in any bigger group.

- ➤ **Same Domain Groups:** If a person joins a group that is similar to their domain, their rivals will be notified. If you want to find future consumers, you should join groups where they are inclined to be. For example, if you are a digital marketer, you should join marketing groups rather than digital marketing groups since those people are more likely to seek your digital-marketing services.

- ➤ **Active Groups:** Always join groups whose members are active; else, your marketing efforts in that group will be unsuccessful.

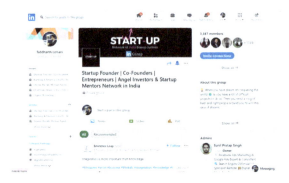

Posting on LinkedIn

Unlike any other platform, posting on LinkedIn is also very easy; you just need to go to the homepage and create a new post as per your requirements; it can be a static post, video, poll, article, and so on.

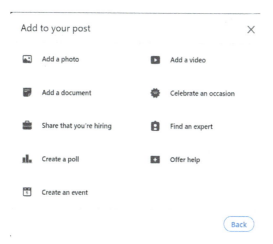

While creating a post make sure that you make ZERO grammatical mistakes as it can hamper your reach also add a maximum of 10 hashtags for better reach and use a combination of hashtags that are from the same domain but contribute to a different topic example: #digitalmarketing #seo etc.

Creation of a company page

For individuals and businesses, it is easy to start posting from your profile, but if you run a company or a business, you should look more professional and take advantage of the amazing free features offered by Linkedin, such as page insights, job posting, content suggestions, post-performance, and many more.

To create a company page, all you require is a good-quality company logo, a brief description, and a few targeted keywords. A LinkedIn description can provide a valid backlink and help you rank higher in search results.

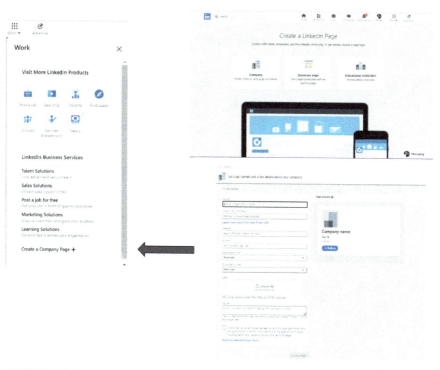

Linkedln campaigns

If you are interested in targeted B2B leads, then LinkedIn can be your go-to platform for marketing.

On LinkedIn, you get a variety of options, such as targeting based on industry, company size, employee role, and many more.

With this, you also get the option to target based on location and other demographics. Remember, LinkedIn ads are comparatively more expensive than other forms of online marketing.

LinkedIn Tips

➢ Use hashtags in your post to maximize reach. Remember to use only post-relevant hashtags.

➢ Use important keywords on your post if it is an image or a video add a caption that has keywords as LinkedIn works as a search engine and categorizes posts, people, companies, and jobs based on keywords.

➢ Join industry-specific groups and share content on regular basis to attract more audience, make the brand name more visible, generate engagement, and garner page likes.

➢ Use the follow-up approach in this you have to contact the prospect 3 times if there has been no response on the previous conversation.

➢ The cheapest ad types are text ads and message ads on LinkedIn. They generally have a low success rate but compared to other forms of ads it is still the best.

➢ Use scrapping tools such as Lusha or apollo.io to generate the email id of the prospect as well as the phone number.

6. YouTube

We are all hooked to our screens, watching content online that can be photos, text, or video. Although compared to all the platforms available, YouTube is the market leader when it comes to video content, as it gives a plethora of options for the user to choose from.

YouTube has niche categories. Educational videos, how-to articles, movies, cartoons, and other media are some examples.

Video content shared on YouTube ranges between 5 and 20 minutes on average, as small bite-size content is preferred more. The YouTube platform has more than 1 billion active users. Youtube offers features such as uploading videos, live streaming and creating playlists.

Best Youtube practices

Following are some of the best practices every marketer should follow to grow constantly on Youtube:-

➢ Be Consistent – Marketers must keep to a schedule such that subscribers know when a new video will be released.

➢ Include a Call-to-Action (CTA) – Request that visitors like, comment, and subscribe to the channel.

➢ Respond — The entire purpose of using social media is to be sociable. Respond to consumer feedback and express gratitude to those that leave comments.

➤ Go Live – YouTube provides a live-streaming tool that marketers may utilize to interact with viewers.

Youtube Content Strategy

Content can help you garner views on YouTube to boost your marketing objectives but it is important to make sure that the content shared is relevant and in demand by the users, or else it won't be helpful. To be certain that the content is curated as per market trends, there are a few pointers to keep in mind:

➤ **Competition analysis:** Before planning out your content close watch on your competitors as to which type of content works for them and helps them to generate views and subscribers. Also, you can search for those topics on youtube search to see the suggestions that may be helpful.

➤ **Find the gap:** If you finalized the topic to make content on try to find out the missing piece that makes the content less informative and form your version accordingly this way you will be assured that your content is fresh and not copied.

➤ **Use tools:** There are various tools helpful for your Youtube journey some are Vidlq, keywords everywhere, and social blade to name a few. Although they are easy to use chrome extensions and web apps you will find a brief about each within this chapter.

➤ **SEO-friendly content**: It's necessary to formulate your content as per the keywords for example the title to be used and the description must have the keywords that are used on youtube and have high search volumes. Creating content with keywords that have no high searches.

Youtube SEO

YouTube favors consistency, but that doesn't mean you have to post any content that has no relevance in terms of SEO. By that, I mean you need to follow a few steps to make your content generate more views and eventually get trending. SEO for YouTube can be easy and has some simple steps to follow.

YouTube, description, On youtube you might get integrated into keyword research on the topic and add those terms in the title, description and tags, though that is not the best strategy to be followed as the first basic step is to finalize a topic, search for similar content on Youtube, thoroughly analyze the keywords used by the creator, find the gap, use similar tags and strategy, and post it.

Here is a step-by-step detailed guide to uploading an SEO-friendly YouTube video:

Make a list of keywords: search keywords on some basic web tools such as vidiq, answer the public, youtube search suggestions, keywords everywhere, google trends, and google keyword planner.

vidIQ is a tool used by YouTube creators to find the tags of the video, the thumbnail used, channel analysis, and keyword research on YouTube. The tool vidIQ is designed to make YouTube publishing easier and to provide extra help and support to creators to increase views and search YouTube views.

Through the picture, you can see that this tool automatically tells the creator about the keyword analysis, such as the difficulty, related keywords, analysis, and top creators of the keyword. From this, you can find out the top videos in which their creators try to shadow their techniques, and that's it.

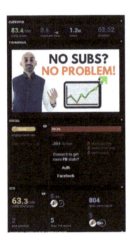

For example purposes, I have opened one video by Neil Patel, and I can analyze some important data for free, such as the tags used and the channel's health. Topics used, channel tags, shares on social media, views count, and the thumbnail used.

Here you can see that the tools assist you while uploading by sharing a real-time Youtube SEO score to ensure it is good. Always add keywords to the title, description, and tags. Not only should they be mentioned, but they should also be consistent across all three sections. No, you don't have to include 30 keywords in your title; just three that are highly relevant should be used across the sections to achieve the best results.

Socialblade

It is an online web application that provides you with more information about a YouTube creator, such as their channel ranking and the estimated monthly or yearly revenue.

It is one of the best tools for any beginning creator to build up some foundations and see what works well in a simple UI that has everything in one place.

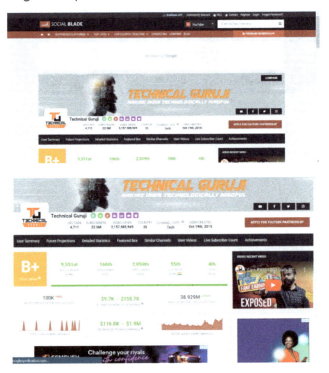

DATE		SUBSCRIBERS		VIDEO VIEWS		ESTIMATED EARNINGS
2022-10-17	Mon	22.5M		3,139,039,417		$0 - $0
2022-10-18	Tue	22.5M	+1,417,163	3,140,456,580		$354 - $5.7K
2022-10-19	Wed	22.5M	+3,652,890	3,144,109,470		$913 - $14.6K
2022-10-20	Thu	22.5M	+1,244,655	3,145,354,125		$311 - $5K
2022-10-21	Fri	22.5M	+1,313,702	3,146,667,827		$328 - $5.3K
2022-10-22	Sat	22.5M		3,146,667,827		$0 - $0
2022-10-23	Sun	+100K	22.6M	+1,437,224	3,148,105,051	$399 - $5.7K
2022-10-24	Mon	22.6M	+2,597,083	3,150,702,134		$649 - $10.4K
2022-10-25	Tue	22.6M	+1,452,871	3,152,155,005		$363 - $5.8K
2022-10-26	Wed	22.6M		3,152,155,005		$0 - $0
2022-10-27	Thu	22.6M	+1,278,832	3,153,433,837		$320 - $5.1K
2022-10-28	Fri	22.6M	+2,508,369	3,155,942,206		$627 - $10K
2022-10-29	Sat	22.6M	+2,043,743	3,157,985,949		$511 - $8.2K
2022-10-30	Sun	22.6M ○ LIVE		3,157,985,949		$0 - $0
Daily Averages ◁		+2.33K		+1,297,642		$324 - $5.2K
Weekly Averages ◁		+23.3K		+9,083,494		$2.3K - $36.3K
Last 30 Days ◁		+100K		+38,929,242		$9.7K - $155.7K

See Full Monthly Statistics   Share on Facebook   Tweet This

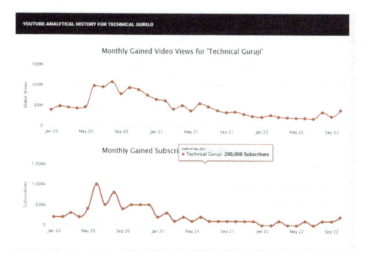

Monthly Gained Video Views for 'Technical Guruji'

Monthly Gained Subscri... ● Technical Guruji: 200,000 Subscribers

Through this analysis, you can make a list of content that has worked for the creator and identify pointers that should be incorporated into the YouTube journey to prevent the account from declining.

And yes, the revenue forecast is something that can spark some competition and make you motivated.

Online tag extractor

While it is recommended to use vidIQ for YouTube, in certain situations, it is not feasible. In those times, a simple online tag extractor tool can save you. For example, https://online-free-tools.com/en/youtube_video_tags_extract_url Using this tool, you can directly see the tags used in the video and copy them easily.

Keywordseverywhere

It's similar to vidIQ but has fewer features compared to vidIQ. It shows tags used in a video as well as the analysis of keywords entered in the YouTube search. But to my surprise, on Google Trends, the suggestions are comparatively better, and it also shows a graph depicting the use of the keyword, just as shown on Google Trends but for YouTube only.

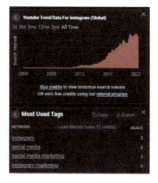

Answer the public

If you don't have a clear idea of what to publish but have a fragmented idea about the content, this tool is surely your best bet. Answer the public's questions. You enter the main keyword for your content into this online web tool, Revolve, and it will show you the most popular keywords around which comparison titles were found in searches. It returns you with questions, predictions, comparisons, alphabetical, questions, and related content.

These terms can further help you finalize your content.

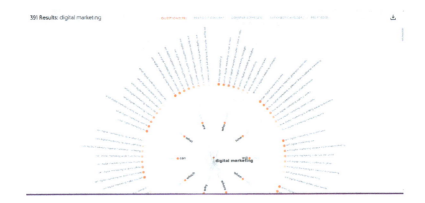

Important tips for Instagram

➢ Before uploading your file on youtube make sure you have renamed the file with the important keyword as it helps in SEO to a certain extent this is because youtube can't watch the content manually a simple signal that is renaming can help youtube decide the relevance.

➢ Make fresh content and find the gap in existing ones. For coming on top of youtube searches remember that youtube favors freshness overview count for search results, so always make fresh content. There can also there be videos that are not talking in depth about the topic or lack information use it as your go-to opportunity as this type of content can garner views by copying their tags and shadowing the content used.

➢ Use eye-catching thumbnails as the more attractive it looks the more clicks you get. Thumbnails that have a sense of question or something surprising tend to do better. For example, a thumbnail such as "The next upcoming Digital marketing trends are?" or "Top 5 tools that are killing your growth on social media". I think you got an idea of what am I talking about so be sure to do some research on various other thumbnails available on youtube by other creators analyze them see what works the best and go ahead.

7. Google ads

It is a platform where businesses could pay to have their websites or other video content appear directly at the top of organic keyword-based search results or web pages.

In layman's terms, you decide which keywords to use to advertise the search engine to find your ad. Only the terms you choose will result in your advertisements appearing.

Google tracks the number of times your advertisements are clicked and charges you for each one. Google also keeps a track of impressions, it is just a figure that indicates how frequently consumers have already seen your advertisement when they searched for that particular phrase.

The click-through rate, CTR is computed by dividing the number of clicks by the number of impressions. This is the proportion of users that clicked on your ad and ended up on the page you promoted.

➤ Maintain keyword consistency throughout the uploading process. By this, I mean the main keyword should be added to the title, description, and tag sections of the video. This helps with the SEO of YouTube and gives the video a strong foundation.

➤ Try to upload a video of not more than 10 minutes in length as the audience as see the duration of the video on the thumbnail and that can be a deciding factor in whether to click and watch the video or skip it. The shorter and more precise it is the more it gets views and hits.

> If you are growing your channel it is important to leverage youtube ads that are done through google ads which will be explained further in the google ads chapter.

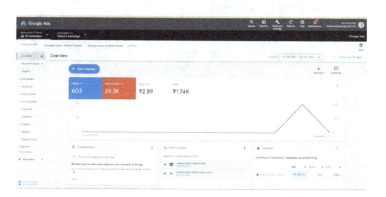

Think of Google AdWords as a marketplace. You set a price and a budget. How much you are willing to spend per click is determined by your bid. If your maximum bid is Rs 80, Google will only show your ad to users if other users aren't bidding more on average.

Google doesn't only want to display the most expensive advertisements, since they may not even be good. They are so concerned about their consumers that they would rather present them with a less expensive, better, and more pertinent advertisement.

Therefore, the winning formula is excellent bid+ quality advertisements!

Search

For example, suppose you are in New York City and someone asks you if you could assist them in locating and recommending some luxury car rentals in New York City so that the next time they relocate to the city, they will have a go-to place for car rentals. In this case, what would you do? Just like any other 21st-century user, you would definitely go to Google and type in "luxury car on rent in NYC" and then choose what's the best based on the reviews and other aspects and maybe pay a visit.

The first 4 results are the ads on Google that local luxury car rentals in NYC created and set up using the Google Ads platform so that they are shown when the user keys in the keyword "luxury car rentals in NYC" or something similar. Such types of results (ads) can be seen above or below the search results of the SERP.

Display

These are banner ads that appear in various sizes throughout the Internet on the websites that your target audience visits. Google Display is the name given to this group of websites. Network. You've probably seen them before. Then some follow you around. When you're browsing the web They are shown to users depending on a variety of criteria and various targeting choices.

Video

Ads that appear in a video that is playing on Google networks or within a video are referred to as video ads. Generally, such ads are seen on Youtube, but people can also find similar ads on sites monetized with Google Adwords. If your objective is to switch from TV to YouTube, this is the most viable option. This ad format is simple to use and effective if you have a limited advertising budget.

Shopping

Marketers, This format is commonly used for e-commerce ads that offer a product. These ads generally appear at the top of the page as shopping ads and are also visible in the shopping tab of Google.

 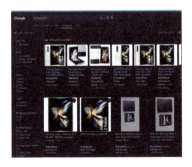

Placement of these ads

➢ Adjacent to search results and separate from text advertisements

➢ Google Search Partner websites, including Youtube

➢ Image Search in some countries

Universal app

Because this app is promoted on Google Play, Google Search, YouTube, and Google Partner Networks (in-app ads and display ads on webpages), it is the go-to ad type for all app marketers. It has two optimization options: app installs and in-app actions.

In google ads you only pay for the results

You have decided the budget for the ad campaign and also allocated funds. You know where to spend Google Ads only charges you when the set action is completed; it can be a click on the link, an action defined by you, reaching 1000 impressions, and so on. In some days, Google Ads can raise your spend by 20% in order to deliver your ads at peak times so they perform better than your competitors'. This way, it makes sure that you don't miss out on certain valuable customer opportunities.

> **CPC/PPC:** Cost per click In this ad type you are charged only when a user clicks on your ad shown on google SERP page or partner networks. It is considered good to use when you want to drive traffic to your website.

> **vCPM:** cost-per-thousand viewable impressions, as the name says, is used to generate product or brand awareness. These are display ads shown on Google partner networks. Google charges you when the ad crosses 1000 impressions and this cycle goes on.

> **CPA:** Cost per acquisition It works in a very targeted manner and only charges you when the user completes a specific task on your website or converts. This is one of the best ad types by google though the setting up of such an ad type can be a little tedious.

Creating your first Search ads campaign

Creation

First, before setting up your campaign, you need to determine the objectives of your ad. This will define the business objective the ad must reach.

> **Sales:** Drive sales online, through apps, over the phone, or in-store. Brand recognition and reach

> **Awareness:** Build a large audience and reach.

> **Leads:** Get more leads and conversions by encouraging customers to participate in the action.

> **App marketing:** Increase your installations, engagement, and pre-registration for your application

- ➢ **Traffic to a website:** Get the correct personnel to come to your house.
- ➢ **Visits to local stores and promotions:** Take drives to local businesses such as restaurants and car dealerships.
- ➢ **Brand and product consideration:** encourage people to investigate your goods or services.
- ➢ **Create a campaign without goal direction:** In this case, you can create a campaign with no goal defined.

Let's assume we are in the first stage of our online marketing, and our objective is to drive traffic to our website. Thus, we choose website traffic.

Here you get an option to choose the ad type; it is always recommended to go with search if you are looking to drive traffic to your webpage. Other options are not required here, as a display ad, for example, will only work in a display campaign, which we will discuss in the next section.

Then you have to choose the bidding type, as Google gives you a few options to choose from when it comes to the cost you are willing to pay as per the objective.

The best viable option here would be clicks, as we are running search ads.

As we have selected the search ad, we don't have to mark other options as it can hinder ad performance. Search and display ads are two different types, and there should be a separate campaign for each type.

Later, we must do some targeting that is entirely based on the location to which we want to show our ads. Further, you can narrow it down to cities and even select the radius. It also gives you the option to select the language you want to target.

Now you are at a very crucial step, which is choosing the keywords you want to bid on. It is always advised to do prior research on keywords before this step using Google's Keyword Planner. It will take you a long time to complete your research. You will come across various keywords based on the search volumes. You again will have to make a decision between choosing broad match keywords, phrase match keywords, and exact match keywords.

In the example, you can see that I have used three types of keywords. Broad match is just mentioning keywords, exact match is within [ ], and phrase match is between " ".

➢ **Broad match keywords:** It's not a viable option for any business to reach out to everyone; it inflates the cost of ad spending as well as fills the pipeline with junk leads. If anyone is searching online and the term somewhere relates to your offering, then your ad will be shown. Here, the user's intent is not clear, and it's only used to understand the workings of Google.

➢ **Phrase match:** As a marketer, you still aren't sure about the keyword users might use, but you do have a little idea. In phrase match, you tell Google to take your keyword as a phrase and show it on the results page when a user searches. For example, your phrase keyword is "chocolate hot tea," so now it will show to users who even search for how to make chocolate hot tea at home that the phrase keyword is intact and only a few words are added that qualify for phrase match.

➢ **Exact match:** If you are definitely sure about what the user will exactly search for, It can be a bit tricky as it highly targets the user's search intent. It can be much more costly than other types but can assure good results.

***There is a feature in Google Ads that is called "negative keywords." This is required to be used if you don't want your ad to show up on a query not related to your business but having identical keywords. For example, you set a phrase match on the keyword "digital marketing courses," but you don't want to appear for the term "digital marketing free course," so you mention it as a negative keyword.*

Ad Level

In setting up a search campaign, this is the only creative step required where you have to write compelling ad copy that can attract the user to click on the ad. The space to write your copy is quite limited, which means you have to be as creative and direct as possible. Below is the pattern you should follow:

It's still advised to create two sets of ads, as every product or service follows a different approach.

This can help you measure what is working better and further optimize it in order to save on your advertising spend.

Optimization

After passing the "under review" status, your ads are displayed on the platform, though that doesn't mean that you are done with the ad setup and will automatically get good results. No matter if the budget is small or large, you are required to check the ad on a daily basis and make certain tweaks to ensure better performance of the ad.

➢ A close watch on the status of your ad is required on the very first day. There might be a chance your ad status shows as "ads disapproved" or "account error." Make sure to follow guidelines laid out by Google to rectify what went wrong, or contact support immediately.

➢ After a few days of running the ad, say 4–7 days, you will receive data from Google indicating which keywords are performing well in terms of impressions, reach, and clicks, as well as which keywords are not performing well in terms of reach, clicks, and so on. In this stage, you are required to give low-performing keywords a tweak by either changing them from exact match to phrase match or pausing them together.

➢ The last stage requires you to make calculated decisions as the advertising budget is being spent daily, and you don't want it to turn out as a waste. Remember at the start of setting up your search campaign it was advised to create more than 2 ads in one campaign to check which is performing better. The standard metric here can be the CTR. Ads with a low CTR should be turned off as they are burning the budget and optimization might not be working that well for those ads.

➢ Optimization is a continuous process that necessitates the marketer's daily efforts. A marketer should never be relaxed after setting up the ad, as it's not a one-day task that requires weeks or even months of effort to make it more relevant and helpful for the business.

Display campaign on google ads

The first stage of any campaign remains the same across all ad types, which is to select a campaign goal. As shown previously, Google Ads will show you a screen of preset ad types, and you have to choose one of them as per your business objectives.

➤ **Sales:** Drive sales online, through apps, over the phone, or in-store. Brand recognition and reach.

➤ **Awareness:** Build a large audience and reach.

➤ **Leads:** Get more leads and conversions by encouraging customers to participate in the action.

➤ **App marketing:** Increase your installations, engagement, and per-registration for your application.

➤ **Traffic to a website:** Get the correct personnel to come to your house.

- ➢ **Visits to local stores and promotions:** Take drives to local businesses such as restaurants and car dealerships.

- ➢ **Brand and product consideration:** encourage people to investigate your goods or services.

- ➢ **Create a campaign without goal direction:** In this case, you can create a campaign with no goal defined.

Here again, we go with the website, which is by far the most convenient and easiest way to boost website traffic. Also, we can capture leads through our landing page or by re-targeting through cookies. Unlike going for a campaign with no goal is a doable option in search ads here it is a strict no.

The next step is to close the campaign subtype.

We go ahead with the standard display campaign.

Next, we have the option to set targeting, generally limited to location and language.

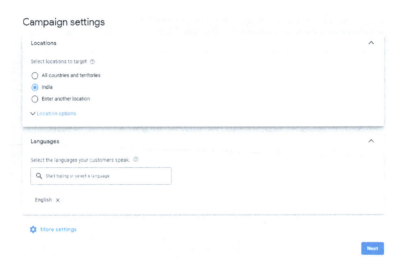

Setting up the audience for the ad is the primary objective of any marketer; for example, you would not like to pay for ads to be displayed in countries outside your target area or to be shown to people who don't speak the language.

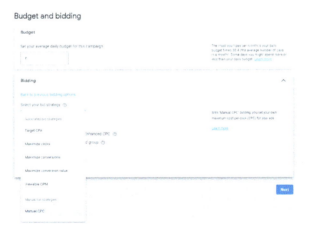

In Google Ads, you get to choose the bidding strategy to maximize your conversions; some of them are listed below.

Bidding strategies

➤ **Target CPC:** Setting bids to achieve the most conversions feasibly.

➤ **Maximize clicks:** By obtaining the most number of clicks within a given budget.

➤ **Viewable CPM (cost-per-mille/thousand):** Obtaining the greatest number of viewable impressions potential (excellent for brand awareness) (good for brand awareness)

➤ **Manual CPC:** If you don't trust Google's automatic tactics and want to put up your own personal Or they are irrelevant to your campaign.

Campaign name	Test display ads	⌄
Campaign status	⏸ Paused	⌄
Goals	Using account goal settings	⌄
Marketing Objective	Website traffic	⌄
Locations	All countries and territories	⌄
Languages	English	⌄
Bidding	Target CPA - ₹10.00	⌄
Budget	₹100.00/day	⌄
Ad rotation	Optimize: Prefer best performing ads	⌄
Start and end dates	Start date: November 8, 2022 End date: Not set	⌄
Devices	Show on all devices	⌄
Frequency management	Let Google Ads optimize how often your ads show (recommended)	⌄
Campaign URL options	No options set	⌄
Dynamic ads	No data feed	⌄
Conversions	Don't include view-through conversions in your "Conversions" and "All conversions" columns	⌄
Value rules	No rule set	⌄
Content exclusions	Show ads on all content	⌄

Settings

After you go through the process of creating ads, which is quite simple and fast, you might not want to make a few more edits in order to make the ad more relevant and limit the spending.

Just like you, I also kept the settings of the ad the same after I published it. But it is suggested that you edit the settings, as they have some options that you are required to explore and modify.

➤ **Start and end dates:** Ads are generally live for a set duration, as the sale or the offer might have set start and end dates. Running ads that have no relevance is like burning money. Make sure you set the dates accordingly to save money.

- ➢ **Frequency capping:** You don't want your ads to be shown to people multiple times and then they do nothing; this will waste your money and make the user lose trust in the company. It is recommended to set the frequency of the ad as it limits impressions per user.

- ➢ **Location:** Showing ads to people that are highly unlikely to take any actions. This can burn through your budget, so it is important to target only those locations that are relevant to your business and locations where your business is operating. In the settings option, you can edit it to get better returns from your ads.

Ad group level

All the basics of the ad have been set up: location, frequency, start date, end date, and so on. The most important of these is the detailed targeting available through the ad group.

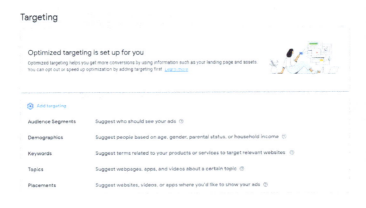

> **Affinity:** The number of audiences you can target can be quite large, so it is important to niche it down based on their interests, such as their interest in technology, a hobby of traveling, and so

on. This can prove to be highly useful as it can further make your ad relevant for the audience.

➢ **Intent:** People who are actively searching for products and considering buying something. These are the people who are likely to take action after seeing your ad, so they are quite important. No matter what their interest lies in, they are more likely to make a purchase compared to other people, and this can be done at the ad group level.

➢ **Re-marketing:** Any interactions people have had in some way with your business can be re-marketed under this option. This can be an effective option as it can increase your leads, conversions, clicks, and so on.

➢ **Demographics:** This helps you target people based on their age, gender, income, and parental status. In a nutshell, this option has to be used while creating your ad as it can prove to be very helpful.

Content targeting

This defines where you want your ad to be shown and exclude people whom you don't want to reach

➢ Placements: Choose a specific platform such as you can pick a specific website niche, video type, and even apps where you want your ad to be shown.

➢ Keywords: It is similar to search where only when the user enters a specific keyword then your ad pops up. In your ad make sure to enter relevant keywords to make the ad visible to the right audience.

Video campaigns

Similar to display ads Video campaigns can be set up easily; you just need to follow the steps for setting up any campaign, but you also need to add a YouTube video link in the ad setup. YouTube is widely used, so video can be a viable alternative to other forms of advertising.

It has been proven that video ads have more relevance compared to any other ad format for various reasons, the most common of which is that videos are easy to understand and communicate more clearly. Video ads also tend to reach the right audience.

Setting up a video campaign

The process is quite simple in the way we set up display ads, but you also have to make sure the video length is appropriate, as a lengthy video can result in more ad burn. Also, a short video ad that is to the point works better; try to have a hook within 5 seconds of the video, and it should not exceed the 25-second mark.

Further,   you
are required to fill out the basic information that is required for every
type of campaign you set up, which includes locations, placements,
budget, and start and end dates.

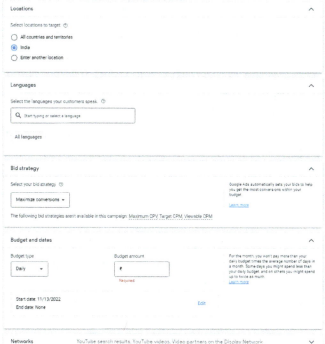

There is a slightly detailed approach to setting up a video campaign. In video ads, you get the option of setting up an audience during set-up.

8. Important Tools and Updates

AI-Powered Optimization

Might look like a heavy term but it's not in simple words it means that artificial intelligence is going to take up the major part of digital marketing here it refers to optimization. In digital marketing, optimization is the key whether it's keywords for SEO, content for blogs and social media, or Ads. Optimizations let the marketer adjust the performance based on the metric received in real-time for example- based on the trends marketer decides the keyword chosen and makes a blog. It is expected that the whole optimization part of digital marketing will be done by AI in the future.

However, we can see some touch of AI in optimization in the present time, for starters marketers extensively use Buzzsumo for their content needs. Buzzsumo crawls down the entire digital space and presents the most trending content to the marketer based on the parameters set. Parameters such as what type of content is the marketer looking for? on which platform? What type of demography is the marketer want to target?

Based on this Buzzsumo provides the data to the marketer and the marketer then easily makes content based on the results got. This reduces the efforts of hours of manual search and the time taken to plot the data based on the research and then come up with something.

Similarly, Google trends are used by marketers to get factual insights on the content based on the preferences of the marketer.

If the above information is not exciting to you then maybe looking at the data generated through primary search might bring out some curiosity in you about the future potential of A.I.

Google Keyword Planner

The main objective of any marketer or business is to bring traffic to the website in order to get more conversions defined by the business. Google keyword planner is a far more sophisticated tool for keyword research as it gives more accurate data and is free. Also a point to note that google is the most used search engine throughout the world, thus always return accurate results.

In google keyword planner you just need to add a word or a phrase and it will give you suggested keywords too that you can use for your ads or SEO.

Uses of Google Keyword Planner

In Google Ads you get two most useful options:

➢ **Find keywords:** Using Google Keywords Planner you get insights on the number of searches in a given duration also it gives you a list of targeted keywords that can be used to generate more more reach among people.

➢ **Insights on search volume and forecast:** See past performance of your keyword also forecast the anticipated results from the keyword.

Canva

It is one tool that every marketer has to be proficient in. Canva can make almost any type of creative PPT, social media post, business card, poster, e-book cover, video, and more.

This book's cover was also designed on Canva. As we all know hiring a designer can be a little expensive thus utilizing a tool that is free and professional requiring no design knowledge can be a good deal.

Furthermore, I would add that you might not find professional vectors in a free edition of Canva for that you can go to www.freepik.com to get vectors and add them to your design.

References

➤ Gupta, S. (2020) "Introduction and Social media," in Digital Marketing. Porur, Chennai: McGraw Hill Education (India) Private Limited.

➤ Krizmanic, A. (2020) Create your first google ads search campaign with ease, Kontra agency. Available at: https://kontra.agency/first-google-adwords-search-campaign-creation/ (Accessed: November 17, 2022).

➤ Log in or sign up (no date) Facebook. Available at: https://www.facebook.com/ (Accessed: November 17, 2022).

➤ Google ads - get more customers & generate leads with online ads (no date) Google. Google. Available at: https://ads.google.com/home/ (Accessed: November 17, 2022).

➤ Instagram. Available at: https://www.instagram.com/ (Accessed: November 17, 2022).